The House Was Quiet, But the Mind Was Anxious

poems by

Nancy Avery Dafoe

Finishing Line Press
Georgetown, Kentucky

The House Was Quiet, But the Mind Was Anxious

*Dedicated to the memory of my son
Blaise Martin Dafoe (1987-2019),
to his loving sisters, my daughters
Colette and Nicole, and his father, my husband Daniel R. Dafoe,
his brothers-in-law, my sons-in-law David and Adam,
and Blaise's nephews, my four little grandsons
Truman, Enzo, Owen, and Luca*

ACKNOWLEDGMENTS

The following were first published:

"After Lightning, Before Thunder" in *The Cortland Standard* newspaper
 "Touching My Face" in *The Pangolin Review* website, COVID-19 issue
"When the Body Tells the Story" in *The Healing Muse*
"Sometimes Loss Weighs Lightly" in *Innermost Sea*
"Gloaming" in *34th Parallel Magazine*

Publisher: Leah Huete de Maines
Editor: Christen Kincaid
Cover Art: Katie Turner
Author Photo: Parker Stone
Cover Design: Elizabeth Maines McCleavy

Order online: www.finishinglinepress.com
                 also available on amazon.com

Author inquiries and mail orders:
Finishing Line Press
PO Box 1626
Georgetown, Kentucky 40324
USA

Table of Contents

After Lightning, Before Thunder

In absence, there is expanse.
I have lost time, not in a sense, as in,
"It's two o'clock already?"

I have lost progression,
timelines and while—
tempo and duration.

Winds beat my doors and windows
and compass can no longer
find true north.

As Dickinson said,
"When everything that ticked
—has stopped—"

After the death of my father,
I thought it was a Tuesday
when Monday entered.

After the death of my mother,
I stepped outside and stared
at setting sun until dawn.

After the death of my brother,
I bent to pick up a small stone
and knew not where I was.

After the death of my son,
I dropped a glass, shattering,
and broke open the immeasurable.

Parallel Delivery on Limits of Sight

A poem already written in the title
of a panoramic photograph by Jamie Young:
"My Mother Sees Her Hill for the Last Time,"
I stop, unsure of where to go
from that place of perfect articulation
both with inkjet photo and caption.

I allow myself to be pulled in,
stand at center of an archival, otherworldly
print suggestive, as my eyes follow paths
of ghostly hillside and trees
walking away from this earth, seeing
moss-covered rocks and knotted lives.

Descending hill in transparency is not choice,
just as dying is not choice for old growth trees
as they become ancient souls
from the perspective of earthly existence.

Each side of this narrow view on gallery wall
shot by and from an intelligent lens
rises from outer edges of my iris,
a parallel delivery on the limits of sight.

Her art at once a photograph and metaphor
for paradoxical limitations
within wide-angle expanse of her mother's life,
our mother's lives, our own lives, the whole
of what it means to be temporal,
moving in mist through new shoots of forest.

The House Was Quiet, But the Mind Was Anxious

The house was quiet, but the mind was anxious
knowing now the world could never be calm.

Even reading at night, and reader struggling with poem,
the house begins to suspect worry, not calm.

The world is fraught, burning in division, then diversion
as thoughts turn inward for protection, not contemplation.

Even reading Wallace Stevens' strangely hypnotic poem,
the house acknowledges disconnect and politic diversion.

Turning pages, no less than turning inward again, anxious
in sleep and waking to agitation, balance broken.

A wasp outside striking screen even in peace of day;
songbird flying at a window, bird now broken.

There was a time when thoughts did not end in disquiet;
when the house was young and without contemplation,

but now experience has opened, splitting peace of day,
and reader closes her eyes, even house knowing disquiet.

African Dwarf Frog Aria

After my son's death, I inherited
his Albino African dwarf frog:
white, pink-eyed creature singing
before I enter his room late.

A vibrato in the middle of the night
more bird-like than the genus'
typical faint buzzing,
this frog's incantation out of love
or loneliness or loss has an unearthly
quality yet so very much of this earth.

Unable to name the frog,
I have no idea if my son had given him
a name, his late-night singing
always striking a core with that high note
of the aria, as if this diminutive opera
singer's performance could be heard
upon some otherworldly stage, too.

To the Greeks, he represented harmony.
Through the ages, frogs have come
to symbolize transformation,
and I indulge myself by thinking
of my son in his changing state
with an animal spirit guide.

Again and again, I hear
a thrilling trill, those high notes
not possible according to the science.
Each time I approach his aquarium,
I am thinking about symbolism of rebirth,
but my looming shadow freezes
the frog's song, and I know
that his music was never meant for me.

Theory of Everything Except

Poet enters austere echo chamber
where TOE—theory of everything
is chalked across expansive blackboards,
equations looking like conglomeration
of chaotic foreign languages, symbols

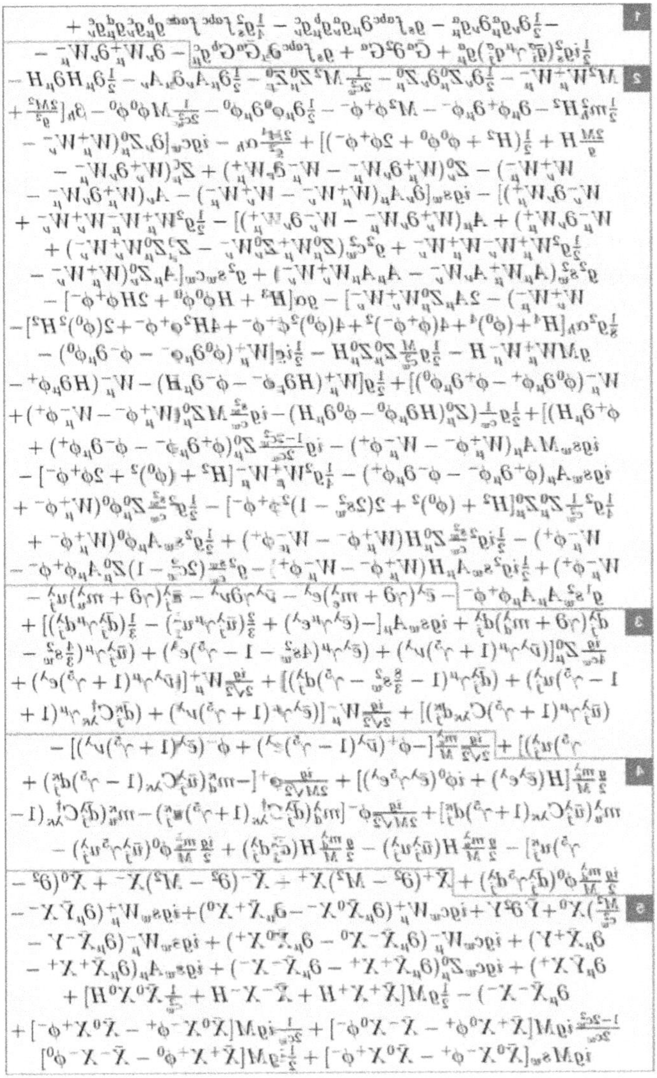

providing framework for how it all fits
together—quantum mechanics, scientific laws
of the universe in play in M-theory,
this leading candidate for explanation
for the seeming inexplicable,
as poet takes mental notes of erasures,
struggling sheets of papers crumpled,
a pair of discarded glasses on side table
next to arguing physicists.

Poet deliberately flips formula orientation,
wondering if altered perspective—
right to left will allow some inkling
of solace in a universe in which
mathematics neatly computes everything
in terms only scientific gods
comprehend—without explanation
for the loss of a single son.

Until the Furies Have Left

To those weary from our sadness,
let bemoaning mothers say what's permissible
in bereavement is more than sorrowing in solitude.

Store away platitudes and ready-made
"thoughts and prayers" banality for those
who care less than mourning mothers.

When we, who have lost our sons and daughters,
lament, we will cry out for the unnatural return
of our children, abducted like Persephone.

Mothers suddenly leaping into fury,
punishing ourselves fiercely like the Erinyes,
snake-like hair writhing in our grief.

Let us who long for beautiful son or daughter
scream and shout, moan and gnash our teeth,
pull away rocks until fingers bleed in breaking.

Allow us to dig deeper into rage,
raving until those wild and violent winds
lift and bear us away.

It is not the dead, but the grieving
who refuse our children going gently
into that good black night.

With Age Comes Urgency

Or is it death's latency, not age
that propels need to hurry, narrow the search?

A nearby nest means hornets are continual visitors,
most flying by overhead or at foot,
a few stopping to warm themselves on wooden dock;
ominous vibrating more than buzzing,
insects circle human intruder.

Welcome wings of a dragonfly patrolling,
hovering above, quiet the wasps momentarily
as fall breezes deceptively cross waters
disguised as mid-summer's exhaling breath.

Even random lines in a woman's journal
are too imbued with portent. Movements
toward poetry or prose latent, scrambled still
as words on a page of paradoxical disassembly,
phonemes circled, reconstructed—
chaos no ordering principle,
urgency in whirring wings.

Your Presence in Silent Rooms

Your presence in silent rooms,
the surprise of you again and again—
comforting, even as the room weeps.

How did I not remark with growing dread?
"His long, slender fingers; his long, slender toes?"
How did I not know what unearthly beauty portends?

My son, I knew so well yet did not know
those gestures you made, those unexpected gifts
of stories told by strangers who knew you, as well.

Mourners filing in, "the patron saint of unwed mothers,"
someone remarked because you were tender, generous
to others who were struggling in deep waters.

An addict in the mourning room, shuffling his feet
in the back, unable to approach. "You did nothing wrong,"
my daughters told him. "He did not die from an overdose."

"He was king of the sauna," another remarked,
uncomfortable, stifling laughter. "Made us all laugh,
made our awful jobs bearable," a dark-haired man said.

Delivered pizza to a boy with cancer every night
after work and never said a word about this kindness;
the boy with cancer living still, but my boy gone.

"He was my best friend," they said again and again,
as if my son had been a dozen men, not one
who sometimes seemed alone and inconsolable.

How could I not have known about these expressions
of benevolence, his political savvy, his quick humor?
How could I not have apprehended he would leave?

We Break and Break and Break

A constellation of bones and muscles, tender
tendons and emotional states, disparate neurons
and delusional divisions, we, fair gender,
fall in wars between states and erotic liaisons.

Our bodies split and birth, trembling and quaking.
We are raped and beaten, belittled. No escape.
Dragged by our hair through hellscape
of mankind's merciless, inventive shaping.

We rise in the morning to flooding, collapsed
by poverty and fears both rational and craven,
to the back of our necks tingling in anticipation;
even the salt in our blood and cells imbalanced.

And always the impermanence of life, our thesis.
Loss looms large—our cognition, our sentience
a curse even as gifted to the human species.
Knowing the break will come, we embrace.

We break and break and break in sorrow,
yet we wake each bright, expectant morning
sanguine and hopeful, to mourning and love
until final clamoring or silent leaving.

You Have No Guide Like Virgil

Sometimes the world's colors are too bright,
and you traverse charcoaled, limited palette of density,
vista or perhaps a seascape if that body of water
is as indeterminate. Foaming, cresting waves
in the distance are nearer than you think
with the partially clouded moon still
above your head, not reflected at your feet
as Dante, the poet, found in unholy descent.

You have no guide like Virgil at your ready
to orient you, lift you as you traverse this achromatic
landscape without purpose of revenge like Hamlet
with his "inky cloak" and "suits of solemn black,"
though your darkness weighs on your shoulders
and shades surround you as intended when,
"all forms, moods, shapes of grief" denote you
as surely as they did Shakespeare's Danish Prince.

Yet, there you are setting out: mystery, rebellion,
fear—questioning immortality in this recognition
of loss, but no cowardice shown on your journey
with shadows as philosophical as Pascal Quignard's
and as immediate as the wounds on your hands, scars
now lost through absorption of visible light. You walk,
knowing there is no predestined path, only suggestion
of horizon, possible break, leading across black without hue.

When you lift your weary head with such effort,
you become aware of presence: those who came before you
on this impossible passage—your past in front of you,
before you comprehend how doubt informs.
In process: becoming, even in your falling away.

If you wake before sunrise,

you will hear Loon long before
you will see bird, its long, high-pitched
wail—plaintive voice reduced
to anthropomorphism: loneliness, sorrow.
Loon's long-distance communication,
asking for mate to locate, also informs
you to physical and emotional locus.
You know what it is to be in sadness
all the way past muscle to bone.

After coffee in the camp, later
in the morning, you have covered
yourself—funny hat, wool jacket,
and set out in a motor boat to find
calling bird, listening for tremolo—
call of stress or alarm after deep dives.
When yodel suddenly breaks quiet, cuts
through dense white fog, territorial
whistling lets other Loons know,
this owned wilderness.

Entering a narrow channel,
trees naked and fallen in your path,
you spot a female bird hooting softly,
short, lower pitched calls, and only
with your binoculars do you see
the fuzzy bit of extra feathers
on Loon's back and then, and only
then are you able to detect loon chick
hitching a ride over dark water
where northern pike await.

Our Blue Water Planet is Burning

Our blue water planet is burning.
Our politics are rife with hate, racism, misogyny,
cruelty toward humans, animals, plants;
even rocks have no safeguard once in human sights.
Empathy and sympathy are as endangered
as the elephant and most of the world's species.

Turning to the sky—
out beyond darkness of man's constructs—
beyond points of light of a passing aircraft,
beyond rotating satellites,
beyond what the naked eye is capable of taking in,
there is extraordinary beauty
observed through Chandra's X-ray Observatory telescope,
launched aboard our Space Shuttle in 1999,
sending images of other worlds, other universes,
triplet black holes, quasars, 3D visualizations
through computer simulations,
oh, and a neutron star pulling in matter,
Dr. Jekyll and Mr. Hyde-named pair
of star and black hole.

Otherness, impossible possible, observed
from our finite world and limited view
made nearly limitless.
Cartwheel Galaxy, 150,000 light years in diameter—
as if we could conceive such distance
from across our small rooms dwarfed
on a blue burning planet.

There is the ultraviolent Helix Nebula,
stellar system Eta Carinae—that volatile system
with two massive stars five million times more luminous
than our sun; Supernova 1987A, we are only viewing
after death of that star, its spectacular million-years-ending
looking like otherworldly fireworks in display
of extraordinary colors, light, and patterns.

Our minds are drawn to glowing rings of hot gas
spreading across galaxies as interstellar clouds
expand and move across time and space,
limitless to the man or woman standing
at the top of staircase become mountain.

Space not black after all, not empty,
but eternal in eruptions of light and matter—
forever beginning anew.

Gravity

He was.
Tensing from this past tense,
I move slowly

like some ancient,
weighed down then
collapsed by grief.

English commands: I am,
I think, I sorrow for my son.
He was; I still am.

Abstractions distract,
making it possible to continue
moving out from paralysis, inertia.

In Gaelic ethos, sadness
is upon me, laying its heavy cloak
over landscape and language.

That poetic syntax,
passive in aspect;
seismic shift is now inside me.

What that means,
what departs, I am bereft
when world tilts on its axis

until something, no, someone
tall and beautiful disturbs it,
stops all motion before being swept away.

I so want to see him
not in photos but here and now,
searching night sky

until my eyes catch the moon
holding oceans; gravity pinning this body,
pulling fiercely downward.

Spinning, earthbound, tethered, I look
for my son further out, out past
a whirling earth, beyond my sight.

Touching My Face

Virus and fear close us in
as we're instructed not to touch our faces.

When she passed a mirror, she turned not recognizing
the woman she saw reflecting 72 years when she
believed she was 32, bringing hands to her cheeks.

When child rubs his nose, tenderly touches chin
with his little fingers, all there, he cries
as he picks himself up after fall down the hill.

Even before a kiss, at love's first blush,
he gently brushes back hair from her forehead,
cradles her face with his large hands.

Even before she writes first word of a poem,
her hands hug her chin in contemplation
as reflection moves toward ideation.

After wars and absences, returning home
is always met with hands on faces,
rediscovering, reacquainting.

The impossibility of no longer touching,
experiencing identities denied.

Waiting for the Cardinal to Return

Waiting for cardinal to return
to fighting reflection in my window.
"Stay at home" directive in midst of pandemic,
listening for whirling whispers and weighted sighs
of roof lifted by wind, or are they sighs
from ghosts of those lost to us?

Stay at home barefoot, padding on familiar,
wrapped in blanket by the fire watching
for the ice to leave, waiting for early arrival
of passing-through birds, diving ducks
on newly agitated water.

Stay at home tracing
changing face of landscape and memories,
some joyful, others wailing, haunting
as they will always be in the places
we bring our babies home and hold them
close; in the places of birth and death.

Stay at home and listen for soft calls
of mourning doves, waiting for impossibility
of return; a beautiful son's stillness
in photograph touched by tentative light.

After Lines Dropped

On the ice, two figures suddenly appear,
tent flap open and flapping in chill wind
over water. Men lumbering in the way
men do through drifts of snow coating
dangerous black ice below, ice waiting
for them to lose their footing in such
awkward trudge across peril where faces
and feet are frozen, fishermen persisting
in search of a new site, pun on sight
lingering as they drill through thick layers
in search of elusive big fish at winter rest.

Men folding up their tent, pulling up
their lines attached to colorful, ineffectual
lures, piling all on a child's sled in search
of a new location to try, drill again
into blackness beneath white snow-covered
lake, in vain or vein, these quiet fish deep,
with slowed heart rates and patient eyes.

I wonder, thinking the effort of fishermen
not unlike the writer's: picking up pen,
parting from whiteness of an unfertile page,
pondering movements away in pursuit
of somewhere spawning words, some locus
where constructs rise up out of the depths,
awakened from their winter rest, somewhere,
oh, somewhere to lay down winter's lines.

Scaling Mid-Ocean Ridges

I

In the midst of writing a memoir about my son,
I am immersed, having made deep, dangerous dives
exploring along sea floor of another realm,
inhabiting that region, scarcely remembering
my long descent, those early struggles to breathe
underwater with my ears popping,
my lungs aching, pressure finally stabilizing,
locus achieved, where words await discovery
in dim light, sunlight filtering down through
murky water, swaying seaweed,
but I remained calm, got my bearings.
Becoming comfortable at those depths,
scaling mid-ocean ridges, noting habitats sculpted
by ancients, by glaciers and shifting plates,
as if I had always been a creature of the sea.

II

When it is time to surface, I feel disoriented,
attuned to nuances of underwater landscape,
of intonation and elucidation that I had seen through
waters as pellucid, dwelling not as explorer
but as inhabitant. Once more on land, I gasp for air,
struggle, squint, adjusting to harsh quality of light,
that other realm still haunting, still calling.
Laying down pen and moving away from keys,
I know this book has ended, my boat tied to shore,
my journey already transposed as memory.
Wandering without destination,
I am struck by eerie silence, silence at every level,
pure structures beneath sight, yet symmetrical.
I will have to learn a new language, new ways to move,
fluency far from tongue or keyboard.

III

At the edge of the woods, just beyond utterance,
something swiftly leaping catches my eye.
Multiverse opening. Ensorcelled by sounds
and shape of what is yet to form.

Faint Trails from the Disappearance

Between lines, below rippling surface,
something or someone has disappeared.

In the draw of mystery lies escape
out of a jail cell, concrete or imagined—
from a maze, Daedalus' elaborate Labyrinth.

Our schemes become symbols for *the Human Condition*,
the way Nemerov portrayed lonely man in motel room,
or Patrick Modiano's sixteen-year-old
Missing Person gone from darkened Paris streets.

Native Americans offered *l'itoi*,
neither ascent nor descent, the transmigration provides
no answers: only faintest trails of dissipating breath,
neither desertion nor avoidance:
gone from here, from now: our terrible liberation.

Witness to a Crossing

Across a 148-foot expanse carved by a river below,
a suspension rope bridge carried those passing
on ichu grasses woven into bundles and cords,
a bridge through the Andes before giving way,
five travelers falling endlessly.

Returning to the *Bridge of San Luis Rey*, I, too,
like Brother Juniper, witness a death, and shuddering,
ask, "why? Why my son?" When he had worked
so hard to rid himself of addiction; when he had
become so generous and kind?

That question regarding the frayed strands
in the rope bridge of life is the subtext
of every written word. Searching for meaning
in optical illusions of refracted light: two suns,
according to the Chinese witness, or a message
in foam kicked up by ocean waves. Statements
from religious texts altered thousands of times
over centuries, some discarded and others kept
for political purposes even when purported
to be the words of a supreme being.

Why those five on the Inca rope bridge when
it gave way? Why the new mayor, at only 36?
Why at that juncture did his tires slide on ice
over the overpass, sending the new father
into the chasm below? Why our need to find
patterns to this randomness? Why did some
go to work early that morning when planes
turned missiles hit the Towers? We who are yet
in the living must bear witness to the fraying
rope strands slowly coming undone.

Each of us at some point crossing that suspension
bridge at precisely the wrong moment. When we
are all still walking, high over those chasms,
our life bridge continually fraying, giving way
with infinity awaiting below.

Rendered in Shadow

From the far end of a gallery room,
I discover Impressionist painting, drawing me
into a nightscape, a murder mystery, tall detective
rendered in shadow on an otherwise deserted city street
of glistening wet pavement throwing back distorted
shapes and diffused light,
a scene where a tragedy had taken place.
I'd left a murder mystery in progress
on my computer at home.

As I step past the room's opening,
moving my compass, Impressionism turned
into abstract art, visual images transformed
into form, absence of color broken into fractured
white and gray, independent of worldly representation,
gradations demanding perspicacity.

Another few steps and altered light, the scene
on the wall then recognized as winter landscape,
ice layering viewpoint of a painting of water at night
as I move to a position nearly parallel to the wall.

Approaching closer and standing still,
I discern, instead, a photograph of a pond,
surface congealed with black algae—
water meal. Deeper shades looming over,
intellectualized as pines stripped of branches,
mistaken former sign still unidentified but
labeled as something misshapen in a wood.

Leaving the museum, I return to my detective—
who was for a time an obscured tree—
searching for clues, recalling a scene,
an Edgar Degas painting of Madame Camus
while losing his sight, Claude Monet fighting
his cataracts, both offering remade vision of a vision;
Rembrandt, Mary Cassatt, and Georgia O'Keefe
struggling with biology as their eyesight, too, waned,
and neoteric brushstrokes were conceived,
our preoccupation with reality distorted,
this percipient diving deep by intent
with visions unattached to sight.

When the Body tells the Story

Woman floored, right hand clutching—
not simply holding—her knee,
position of her awkwardly bent fingers
show tension even more than her weary,
wary look out of one eye, the other covered
by shock of reddish-brown wild hair
against bright green, indeterminate background
there for contrast in mood and tone,
as well as coloring, there to absorb the blows.

Demarcation, scar on her forehead
between her eyebrows suggests her troubles
started long ago, even before
this latest incident after which she slumped
to the ground, defeated but not done,
her gaze intense,
not looking at anyone but everyone;
her mouth open,
not in the way that models are instructed
in order to appear suggestive, open
as if about to speak, but words refuse to form—
too hard to say what needs to be said.

Oil on canvas too real, too raw to be a painting
except we know,
we see loss in lack of definition
of her legs,
distorted by angles
and blues,
her blues,
now ours.

What We Leave Behind

With last of falling leaves, snapping turtles
and bank beavers leave unmistakable trails
where lake has receded from shoreline.

Following long, wide indentations,
your eye takes you into deeper water
where scant evidence disappears.

Unconcerned about legacies
or immortality, the natural world
offers up its burdens and waning traces.

East of the beaver's fading signature
markings, an aging woman's hand moves;
lines not flawless, yet evidence of pressing intent.

Why Didn't I Cripple Death?

Why did I do nothing when death came for him?
Why did I let strangers remove his body?
Why did I watch in silence,
rather than launch primal scream?

I held my breath and waited—
with churning stomach and caught vowels—
for death to enter. Why did I do nothing?

We love so deeply, so deeply and impossibly
because we cannot stop death from coming.
Because we perish and perish and must watch
those we love given unto death.

Why did I allow him to die?
I hold no sway, no jurisdiction
over unrepentant death who will
arrive unannounced and carry us along.

Empathy

Knowing a congressman's son—
a brightest light, a young man
with sharpened mind and promise—
would close all the doors and windows
of his life while you watch him
helplessly, just as someone's daughter
catches your attention and eye,
beautiful girl momentarily distracted,
losing control of her car as she flies
through the windshield
only to come back broken.

As necessary as it is for our survival,
empathy lays us out, still breathing.

Sometimes Loss Weighs Lightly

Absence
of hummingbird nest from thinnest
of pine branches overhanging the porch
where—if I sit quietly—
she seems to spontaneously appear,
hover near my face, dart sideways,
then settle onto lichen and spider silk nest.

Two chicks' spiked bills straight up,
like blackened toothpicks
jabbing air
until she arrives and offers bounty.

Absence
nothing at all like the time I gathered photographs
of my father who lay in his coffin,
congratulating myself on how I'd held it together
until I picked up his well-worn Syracuse cap.

Nothing at all like my brother's deepest dive,
or the way I felt when the Sherriff had to break
windows in my aunt's house to find her body,
or my mother mouthing words no longer hers.

Absence
nothing like the moment my son could not wake,
nothing whatsoever like seeing his shoes in the entrance
he would never walk through again.

Two summers the hummingbird had come
and made her nest in my tree,
but I haven't seen her since—
even if I waited patiently all day and night.

Sometimes loss weighs lightly,
but it always weighs.

Mortals

Above valleys of the sleeping,
red flag weather fuels the fires.

Their ache begins: individuals,
20 feet tall, amongst towering
80-foot specimens of elder Coulter pines,
groaning against furnace blast tangling
blue-green needles and dark-gray limbs
with other deeply furrowed voices
attesting to anguish in crackle
of arriving sparks.

Wind insinuates itself
then pulls flame further up
from white bark and scrub pines
into heart of prodigious mortals,
who sweat resins,
their jigsaw covering thin and flaky
before fires disassemble these puzzles:
180-foot Jeffrey, gargantuan Sugar Pines,
these old ones drop their woody cones
that hit without sound on ashen earth,
all consumed in the blaze below,
as the Jeffrey registers its last fullness
in futile fight for life:
a long, low hiss,
then aching, stretched-out syllable,
almost spoken word,
articulated
in its burning.

Gloaming

Dusk creeps in slowly at that petty pace
like tomorrows woven by Shakespeare's
Macbeth. Here in this dislocation,
reoccurring shades assume dominance
over objects and faces,
bringing losses to the fore.

Moving without compass, navigating
this half-light as subtext, the past entering
in the umbra in which my mother
stands before her image in a mirror
and does not recognize herself,
dementia clouding sight.

Ghosts of traumas wash over us
without clear delineation. Visions
arriving as if on a late train; memories
flooding the tracks. Sense of place remains
ambiguous. Gloaming on the tongue
and skin: wet, latent.

Unlike the dazzling sun of midday,
borderless dusk brings unease and anxiety
as passengers. Sorrow and guilt lurk,
menacing as phantoms. Always aware
of altered light in this silencing landscape,
in this domain of myth and superstition.

Even the efficacy of language is suspect here;
movement at the periphery without clear lens:
self-deception. Yet where melancholy
and doubt reign, presence below utterance
reminds not only of what has been
but what could yet be, of possibilities.

Afternoon Rains

Haze marks landscape, and earth is drenched
with rain. Already carefully manicured lines
have fallen away although someone has finally
finished her dissertation on cultural approbation
of intellectual affairs, leading to speculations
amongst an increasingly smaller group,
but who will remember?

In a few years, the King has made his way
through the guts of a beggar or something
along those lines as Shakespeare penned,
that esteemed author whose name we all know
but whose works suggest a lifeline in language
flowing like that wanted stream across pages
when someone somewhere opens again
with a quotation from the Bible, the Torah,
The Koran or Quran, The Babylonian Talmud,
The Upanishads, The Bhagavad Gita,
The Ramayana, The Brahmana, Tao Te Ching,
The Puranas, The Samhita, The Samaveda—
human imagination never more furiously at work
than inventing iterations on immortality.

Angry gods mollified by compassionate ones,
all stating it does not end with death, but Dante's
fantastic poetry showing circles of Hell in the *Inferno*
far more limitless than those lines in Paradiso.

As if immortality is no more than split-seconds
in the chaos of innumerable bytes traveling
across time, almost as if we are our gods.

Outside, it is raining.

Love Endures in Ways You Never Imagined
(a duplex)

Love endures in ways you never imagined when you were young.
You should only have to carry your child into this world.

You should never have to carry your child from this world.
An old woman said, "take your pain and make something beautiful."

The old woman said, "take your pain and make something beautiful."
When your daughter was born, you thought the world too small to
hold such love.

When your first child was born, you thought the world too small to
hold such love,
then your second daughter's birth surprised you, revealing love is
boundless.

When your second child surprised you, revealing love is boundless,
you recalled those nights falling for the boy, become man, become
husband.

After you fell so deeply for your dark-haired boy, become man,
become husband,
you found your hearts welcoming your third, a son, who said simply,
"I'm here."

When your beautiful son was born, you felt the earth shake; he said,
"I'm here."
Love endures in ways you never imagined when you were still
young.

With Thanks

A grateful acknowledgement of my publisher Finishing Line Press and Leah Maines, Kevin Maines, and Christen Kincaid for helping me navigate these waters to publishing.

I would also like thank artist Katie Turner for her cover art that continues to inspire me. My deepest appreciation goes out to my poet/writer friends who have read many iterations of the poems in this chapbook and offered comment: Janine DeBaise, Judith McGinn, Mary Gardner, Karen Hempson, and Bobbie Dumas Panek. As always, my gratitude to my ever-supportive husband Daniel and my sister Phyllis Ann Avery and sister-in-law Marilyn Avery, and to my generous, loving daughters Colette and Nicole, my first readers.

"Theory of Everything Except" graphic of partial, "inverted" formula of TOE is the Lagrangian standard model.

"The House Was Quiet, But the Mind Was Anxious" is both homage and response to Wallace Stevens' poem "The House Was Quiet and The World Was Calm."

"Love Endures in Ways You Never Imagined" is patterned after Jericho Brown's new poetry form the duplex.

In addition, I would like to thank masterful poets Carolyne Wright and Gwynn O'Gara for reading my work and providing me with short reviews for the back cover of this book.

Author and educator **Nancy Avery Dafoe** won the Faulkner/Wisdom Creative Writing Competition in poetry (2016). Writing across genres, she has thirteen published books of fiction, nonfiction, and poetry. Her poetry chapbooks and book include *The House Was Quiet, But the Mind Was Anxious* (2022); *Innermost Sea* (2018); and *Poets Diving in the Night* (FLP, 2017). Dafoe has books on education and writing published through Rowman & Littlefield Education: *Breaking Open the Box, A Guide for Creative Techniques to Improve Academic Writing and General Critical Thinking* (2013); *The Misdirection of Education Policy, Raising Questions About School Reform (2016); and Writing Creatively, A Guided Journal to Using Literary Devices* (2014).

She also has two published memoirs: *An Iceberg in Paradise, A Passage Through Alzheimer's* (SUNY Press, 2015); and *Unstuck in Time, A Memoir and Mystery on Loss and Love* (Pen Women Press 2021).

Her published fiction includes a novella, *Naimah and Ajmal on Newton's Mountain* (FLP, 2021), a novel, *Socrates is Dead Again*, and three literary murder mysteries in her Vena Goodwin series: *You Enter a Room* (2017); *Both End in Speculation* (2018); and *Murder on Ponte Vecchio* (Rogue Phoenix Press, 2020).

Her poetry and prose work also appear in numerous magazines, journals, and anthologies, including *Lost Orchard* (SUNY Press, 2014), *Lost Orchard II* (Pen Women Press, 2021), and *New York Votes for Women: A Suffrage Centennial Anthology* (Cayuga Lake Books, 2017), and *The Comstock Review* and *34th Parallel Magazine*. Her writing has earned regional and national honors including first place in the Soul Making Literary national competition in prose poetry and first place in the New Century Writers story, international competition for her story "Piltdown Man." She is the National League of American Pen Women (NLAPW) Second Vice President and member of the NLAPW CNY Branch.

Currently teaching writing workshops through her online business dafoewritingandconsulting.com, Dafoe previously taught writing and English at the high school and community college levels. She lives in Homer, New York with her husband Daniel.

www.ingramcontent.com/pod-product-compliance
Lightning Source LLC
LaVergne TN
LVHW041327080426
835513LV00008B/623